Everything You Lose Creates Space for Everything You Need

Finding Clarity, Courage, and Possibility in Life's Changes

Shyamankar Singhari

Everything You Lose Creates Space for Everything You Need

Finding Clarity, Courage, and Possibility in Life's Changes

For permission requests, please contact the publisher at:

wkrishind.in or contact@wkrishind.in

ISBN: 978-81-992623-7-9

Published by: WKRISHIND.in

Dedication

To all those who have faced loss, felt the ache of empty spaces, and yet found the courage to keep moving forward.

May this book remind you that every ending carries the seed of a beginning.

Acknowledgments

Writing this book has been a journey of reflection, growth, and gratitude. I want to thank:

- **Sarah**, whose story inspired this narrative — though fictional, her experiences reflect the truths of many lives.
- **Family and friends**, for their patience, encouragement, and quiet support that made this work possible.
- **Readers**, who will carry these lessons into their own lives; your courage to face loss is what gives this book its meaning.
- **Mentors**, teachers, and guides, whose wisdom in writing, mindfulness, and personal growth shaped my understanding of resilience.
- **Finally**, to life itself, for its challenges and gifts, for the spaces it opens, and the possibilities it allows.

This book is dedicated to the journey — the endings, the beginnings, and everything in between.

Preface

How to Use This Book

Life is filled with loss. Some losses are obvious: the end of a relationship, the passing of a loved one, the closing of a career chapter. Others are quieter: the fading of friendships, the letting go of old habits, the closing of doors you didn't even notice were there.

This book is designed to help you navigate those losses — not to erase the pain, but to find the space within it for growth, clarity, and renewal. It combines:

- **Sarah's Story**: A journey of loss, discovery, and transformation. Her experiences provide a mirror for your own challenges, showing how loss can be reframed as opportunity.
- **Reflection & Workbook Exercises**: Practical prompts to help you process emotions, explore your needs, and take small steps toward personal growth.
- **A 30-Day Guided Practice**: A structured plan to integrate the lessons from Sarah's story into daily life. Each day includes reflection, journaling, and an actionable step to help you live forward.

How to Read This Book

- **Sequentially or Selectively**: You may read the narrative first, then move into the workbook and 30-day plan, or jump directly to exercises that resonate most with your current experience.
- **Take Your Time**: There is no rush. Reflect on prompts, try actions at your own pace, and return to sections whenever you need guidance or inspiration.
- **Engage Fully**: Writing, drawing, or taking small actions amplifies the benefits of reflection. Don't just read — do.

This book is an invitation: to notice the spaces left behind by loss, to embrace them, and to create a life aligned with your deepest needs. It is both a mirror and a map — showing you where you've been and pointing toward where you can go.

May it guide you gently, inspire courage, and remind you that every loss creates space for everything you truly need.

Introduction

Sarah's Story & Invitation

This is Sarah's story – but it could also be yours. At thirty-two, Sarah thought she had life figured out: a steady job, a cozy apartment, friends she trusted. Then, in a single year, she lost it all: her job, her home, her relationships.

At first, she saw these losses as failures. But slowly, she discovered something profound: every loss creates space for what you truly need.

This book follows Sarah's journey through loss, growth, and renewal. It includes reflections, exercises, and a 30-day guided practice so you can explore your own losses, embrace the space they leave, and step forward into a life aligned with your authentic self.

As you read, let Sarah's story guide you to see your own losses not as endings, but as openings to rediscover who you are and what you need.

Table of Contents

PART I

SARAH'S JOURNEY

Chapter 1

The Weight of What Was

Sarah had always believed her job defined her. It wasn't just a paycheck or a place to spend her weekdays — it was the anchor of her identity. At thirty-two, she wore her title as a marketing coordinator like a badge of honor. She was the one her friends turned to for resume advice, the one her parents proudly introduced at family gatherings, the one who thrived on deadlines, late-night brainstorming, and the thrill of a campaign's success.

Then, with a single email, it was gone.

Her company merged with a larger firm, and "redundancy" became the word stamped across her future. At first, Sarah tried to shrug it off. Layoffs were common; people bounced back. But in the silence of her empty calendar, she realized it wasn't just her job she had lost — it was her sense of who she was.

For weeks, she woke each morning with the same thought: *Who am I now?*

Her days stretched before her, shapeless and foreign. She scrolled job boards, but each listing felt hollow. She attended networking events, forcing smiles and handshakes, but inside she carried the ache of disconnection. The people around her seemed purposeful, driven. She felt like an outsider to her own life.

The weight of what was — her past identity, her former rhythm — pressed down so heavily that she couldn't yet imagine what might come next.

The Hidden Layers of Loss

When we lose something central to our lives — a career, a relationship, a role we've played for years — the pain is not only in the absence itself, but in the unraveling of the identity tied to it. Sarah's job loss wasn't just about money or routine; it was about the pride, validation, and security she had built around that role.

This is why loss feels so heavy. It's rarely a single thread being pulled. It's the whole tapestry shifting.

Sarah noticed this in small, unexpected ways:

- No one asked her about "the next campaign" anymore.
- Her inbox, once overflowing, sat quiet.
- Even her daily commute, with its familiar stops and bustling rhythm, disappeared.

Loss shows us not only what we had but how deeply we tied ourselves to it. And in that revelation, uncomfortable though it is, lies an opening.

Sarah's Turning Point

One afternoon, sitting at her kitchen table with the blinds half-drawn, Sarah opened an old journal. She hadn't written in years. The first entry was from college, full of dreams and unfiltered honesty. As she flipped through the pages, she lingered on a note scribbled in the margin: "*One day, open a bakery.* A *place that feels like home.*"

She laughed bitterly at first. A *bakery*? She had followed a "responsible" path instead — steady work, good benefits, predictable steps forward. But as she sat with the thought, something stirred. Losing her job, painful as it was, had stripped away the excuse that she was "too busy" to dream. For the first time in years, she had space.

And that space was terrifying. But it was also possibility.

Reflection for You

Loss is never just about what's gone. It's also about what it reveals. Like Sarah, you may find that beneath the surface of what you lost, there are old dreams, neglected desires, or deeper questions waiting to be noticed.

Exercise: Naming the Loss

- Think of a loss you've faced — a job, a relationship, a plan that didn't unfold.
- Write down what it meant to you. Was it security? Love? Purpose? Identity?
- Then, like Sarah, ask: *What might this loss be making room for?*
    - Don't rush for answers. Sometimes the gift of the question is enough.

The First Crack of Light

Sarah didn't wake up the next day with her life figured out. Healing didn't come in a sudden burst. But that small act of journaling shifted something inside her. She realized her loss, as heavy as it was, had created a kind of spaciousness she hadn't allowed herself in years.

The weight of what was would always matter — her job had shaped her, taught her, given her pride. But it was not the only story she could live.

Loss is often the end of something we never imagined ending. But it can also be the beginning of something we never dared to imagine starting.

For Sarah, the bakery was still only a dream, a fragile idea on paper. But by writing it down, she honored it. By acknowledging her loss, she began to release its weight. And by releasing that weight, she made space — space for what she might truly need.

Chapter 2

Holding On Too Long

Sarah's apartment wasn't just four walls and a roof. It was her first real home — the place where she'd celebrated promotions with champagne on the balcony, cried on the couch after breakups, and filled the kitchen with the smell of cinnamon pancakes on lazy Sunday mornings.

Every corner held a memory. The window by her bed where she watched the sunrise. The dent on the coffee table from a game night gone rowdy. The little garden of succulents on the sill that had survived more seasons than some of her friendships.

So when her landlord announced a rent increase that pushed the apartment beyond her budget, Sarah didn't just feel financial strain. She felt betrayal, grief, and a desperate urge to hold on.

"Maybe I can pick up extra freelance work," she told herself. "Maybe if I cut back on groceries, or stop going out, I can make it work."

For months, she clung to that thought. She avoided looking at new places, avoided running the numbers that didn't add up. Each rent check she wrote left her bank account gasping, but the idea of letting go — of walking away from the space that had become part of her — felt unbearable.

The Illusion of Safety

Why do we hold on so tightly, even when something is hurting us?

For Sarah, the apartment wasn't just about shelter. It symbolized stability, adulthood, independence. Leaving it felt like losing those things too.

But safety built on what no longer fits isn't real safety. It's a cage disguised as comfort.

Sarah noticed this in subtle ways:

- She couldn't sleep at night, worrying about money.
- She avoided opening bills, the fear of numbers pressing like a weight on her chest.
- She turned down social invitations because she couldn't afford dinners out anymore.

Her home, once a refuge, had become a source of quiet resentment. Still, she resisted change.

The Breaking Point

The turning point came one late evening in winter. Sarah sat at her kitchen table, surrounded by unopened envelopes. She felt a tightness in her chest she couldn't ignore.

She picked up her journal — the same one she'd rediscovered after losing her job — and wrote a single question: *Why am I holding on?*

The answer surprised her: *Because I don't want to admit that chapter is over.*

Tears spilled as she wrote the next words: *But maybe it is. And maybe that's okay.*

Something shifted that night. She began searching for new apartments, not with enthusiasm, but with a quiet willingness. Weeks later, she stood in a smaller place on the edge of town — fewer windows, less charm, but also less weight. For the first time in months, she felt her breath come easier.

And then something unexpected happened: she discovered a patch of community gardens nearby. Curious, she rented a small plot and started planting tomatoes and herbs. It wasn't her old balcony, but it was something new — a different kind of homecoming.

Letting Go as Liberation

What Sarah learned was simple but profound: letting go is rarely just about the thing itself. It's about releasing the grip of fear, nostalgia, and identity tied to it.

Sometimes we hold on so tightly that we don't see the cost. Staying in the apartment cost Sarah her peace of mind, her financial stability, and even her joy. By clinging to the past, she delayed the freedom that came with embracing change.

The truth is, holding on too long drains us. Letting go, while scary, creates space for something better — not always immediately, but inevitably.

Reflection for You

Think of something you may be holding on to: a relationship, a habit, a job, a memory, an old dream. Ask yourself honestly:

- Why does it feel safe to keep this?
- What is it costing me — emotionally, financially, spiritually, physically — to keep it?
- What would I gain, or at least make room for, if I let go?

Exercise: Releasing the Anchor

- Write down one thing you're holding on to that no longer serves you.
- List two reasons it feels comforting or safe.
- List two costs of holding on.
- Choose one small step toward release — donate an old item, have a hard conversation, or write a goodbye letter you never send.

Like Sarah with her apartment, you don't have to leap into the unknown all at once. But each small release loosens the anchor. Each step gives you back a piece of your freedom.

A Lighter Heart

Moving into her smaller apartment didn't erase Sarah's grief for her old home. She still missed the balcony, the light through the bedroom window, the memories etched into those walls. But as she unpacked boxes in her new place, she noticed something she hadn't felt in months: relief.

Relief is what waits on the other side of letting go. Relief, and the possibility of something new.

For Sarah, that something new grew in the soil of a garden. For you, it might grow in the soil of a conversation, a habit, a dream, or simply the courage to begin again.

Letting go is not betrayal. It's permission — permission to step into the life that fits who you are becoming, not just who you were.

Chapter 3
The Quiet of the Void

When Emma, Sarah's closest friend, announced she was moving across the country for a new job, Sarah smiled and said all the right things.

"I'm so happy for you!"
"You're going to love it there."
"We'll FaceTime all the time."

But inside, she felt hollow.

Emma wasn't just a friend; she was Sarah's anchor. Every Saturday morning they met for coffee at the corner café, swapping stories and laughter over oat lattes. Emma had been there through Sarah's breakup, through her job loss, through the long nights when everything felt heavy. Their friendship was woven into Sarah's sense of home.

And then, almost overnight, the rhythm was gone. No more Saturday coffees. No more impromptu movie nights. No more knock on the door with takeout in hand when Sarah didn't feel like cooking.

At first, Sarah filled the absence with distractions. She scrolled endlessly on her phone, binge-watched entire seasons of shows she barely remembered, and signed up for activities she didn't care about just to avoid the silence.

But no matter how she tried to fill it, the void remained.

The Fear of Emptiness

Loss leaves behind silence. A gap. A space where something used to be.

And most of us fear that space. We rush to cover it up, to stuff it with noise, busyness, or new attachments. We think, *If I can just keep moving, I won't feel the ache.*

Sarah realized this when, one evening, her phone battery died mid-scroll. She sat there in the dim glow of her apartment, restless, almost panicked. Without the distraction, the quiet pressed in around her.

She thought: *This is unbearable.*

But then she asked herself: *What if I don't run from it?*

Choosing Stillness

The next night, Sarah tried something different. She turned off her phone on purpose. She sat on her couch, the silence heavy at first. Her thoughts rushed in — memories of Emma, worries about the future, the sting of loneliness. She almost gave in, reaching for the remote.

But then she noticed something: the quiet wasn't empty. It was alive.

Her eyes drifted to a box of old art supplies she hadn't touched since high school. On impulse, she pulled them out. She dipped a brush into watercolor paints and began to move it across the page. Shapes and colors emerged, imperfect but freeing. Hours slipped by.

When she looked at the clock, it was past midnight. She hadn't thought about her loneliness once in those hours. She had been fully present, absorbed, alive.

The void had become a canvas.

The Gift of the Void

What Sarah discovered is something many of us overlook: the emptiness left by loss is not just a hole. It is an opening.

The void is where rediscovery happens. It's where the noise quiets enough for us to hear our own voice again.

When you stop filling every silence, you may notice:

- Forgotten passions resurfacing.
- Ideas bubbling up that you didn't know you had.

- A sense of peace that doesn't depend on external noise.

The void can feel frightening, but it is also fertile.

Reflection for You

If you've experienced loss, you may feel the urge to fill the space it leaves behind. But what if, like Sarah, you allowed yourself to sit with it?

Exercise: Sitting with the Void

- Set aside ten minutes. Turn off your phone, computer, and TV.
- Sit somewhere comfortable. No distractions — just you.
- Notice what arises: emotions, memories, restlessness.
- Write down one thing you discover in that quiet space. It might be uncomfortable, but it might also be surprising — an old interest, a longing, or simply the realization that silence doesn't break you.

A Different Kind of Fullness

Sarah didn't stop missing Emma. She still wished for their Saturday mornings together.

But she also found that the space Emma left behind wasn't only loneliness. It was also possibility.

The watercolors led to more painting. Painting led to joining a local art class. The art class led to new acquaintances – not replacements for Emma, but connections that reminded Sarah she wasn't alone.

In the end, the void didn't take from her. It gave. It gave her back a part of herself she had lost in the busyness of life.

The quiet of the void isn't something to fear. It's something to enter with courage. Because what feels like emptiness at first may turn out to be the richest space of all.

Chapter 4

Finding What Matters

When Sarah first lost her job, her apartment, and even the comfort of her weekly coffee dates with Emma, her instinct was to rebuild exactly what she had lost.

She spent hours on job boards, searching for roles that mirrored her old marketing position. She bookmarked apartments that looked like her former home – open windows, little balconies, modern kitchens. She even joined online groups, hoping to find a friend who could fill the exact shape of the void Emma had left.

But every attempt left her unsatisfied.

"I thought I knew what I wanted," she wrote in her journal one night, frustration pressing heavy on her chest. "But the more I chase it, the emptier I feel."

It wasn't until she walked into a small neighborhood bakery one rainy afternoon that something shifted.

The Unexpected Spark

The bakery wasn't remarkable at first glance. The paint on the sign was chipped, and the chairs wobbled a little when she sat down. But as Sarah bit into a warm croissant and watched the baker laugh with a customer across the counter, she felt a quiet joy she hadn't felt in months.

It wasn't about the pastry. It was about the atmosphere — the smell of fresh bread, the chatter of people greeting each other by name, the sense of belonging that hung in the air.

Something inside her stirred. She remembered her college journal, the scribbled dream of "owning a bakery one day." She had always pushed it aside as impractical. Too risky. Too uncertain.

But in that little bakery, with rain tapping against the window, she realized something: maybe what she needed wasn't to replace what she lost. Maybe what she needed was something altogether different — something that fed her soul, not just her résumé.

Wants vs. Needs

For weeks, Sarah wrestled with the difference between what she wanted and what she truly needed.

She had wanted her old job back — the title, the validation, the steady income. But what she needed was purpose.

She had wanted her old apartment – the big windows, the memories etched into its walls. But what she needed was stability and peace.

She had wanted another Emma – someone who could fill the hole left by her friend. But what she needed was connection, even if it looked different from before.

Wants are often shaped by habit, expectation, or fear. Needs come from deeper within – from the quiet voice that knows who you really are.

The challenge is slowing down long enough to hear the difference.

A Brave Step

Sarah didn't quit everything and open a bakery the next day. The idea was too big, too fragile, to jump into all at once. But she took one small step: she applied for a part-time job at the very bakery she had visited.

It wasn't glamorous. The pay was modest. Her friends raised eyebrows: "You're overqualified for that."

But Sarah didn't care. The first time she tied on an apron and stepped behind the counter, she felt alive. She kneaded dough, learned the rhythm of ovens, and inhaled the sweet scent of cinnamon rolls at dawn.

For the first time since her job loss, she felt she was moving toward something — not just away from what she had lost.

That one step led to another. She signed up for a culinary course at a local college. She started sketching ideas for recipes in her journal. She began to imagine what her own bakery might look like.

She didn't have all the answers. But she had a direction. And that was enough.

Reflection for You

When loss strips away what you thought you wanted, it's natural to try to rebuild the same picture. But sometimes the gift of loss is the chance to see what you truly need.

Exercise: Defining Your Needs

- Write down three things you want right now (e.g., a new job, a partner, a home, financial success).
- For each, ask: Why do I want this? What feeling or value am I chasing?
    - A job may represent stability or recognition.
    - A partner may represent love or belonging.

    - A home may represent safety or freedom.
- Circle the deeper need underneath the want.
- Choose one small action you can take to honor that need — for example, write a gratitude list for stability, call a friend for connection, or declutter a corner of your home for peace.

What Matters Most

Sarah's journey wasn't about croissants or career changes. It was about discovering what truly mattered to her.

Loss had forced her to strip away the noise — the titles, the appearances, the expectations. In the quiet that remained, she discovered purpose, joy, and a new path forward.

And that path wasn't about recreating her old life. It was about creating the life she actually needed.

When we stop chasing what looks good from the outside and start listening to what feels true on the inside, we begin to align with what matters most.

For Sarah, it was the smell of bread rising in an oven. For you, it may be something entirely different — a cause, a craft, a connection. Whatever it is, loss can clear the space for you to find it.

Chapter 5
The Flow of Loss and Gain

By the time Sarah was taking culinary classes and working part-time at the bakery, she had begun to notice a pattern.

It wasn't just about losing her job or moving apartments or saying goodbye to Emma. Each time something had been taken from her, something new had eventually arrived. The timeline wasn't immediate, and it wasn't painless, but it was undeniable.

Her job loss had felt devastating. Yet without it, she would never have reopened her journal, rediscovered her dream, or dared to step into a bakery kitchen.

Her apartment loss had felt humiliating. Yet without it, she wouldn't have freed herself from the crushing weight of rent or found the community garden that gave her grounding.

Her friend's departure had left her lonely. Yet without that quiet void, she wouldn't have picked up a paintbrush or joined an art class where new friendships were quietly forming.

Each ending was also a beginning.

Seeing the Pattern

One evening in her new apartment, Sarah spread a roll of craft paper across her table. She began to draw a timeline of her life, marking major moments of loss – the breakup with her college boyfriend, the death of her grandmother, the layoff, the move, Emma's departure.

At first, the paper looked like a litany of heartbreaks. But then she added what came after: the ways each loss had shaped her, the gifts each had eventually given.

She realized that without the heartbreak of her college relationship ending, she never would have traveled abroad alone and discovered her love for new cultures. Without her grandmother's passing, she might never have learned the importance of family stories, or started recording them. Without Emma moving, she might never have rediscovered painting.

The pattern was clear: loss and gain weren't separate. They were threads of the same fabric.

The Dance of Life

Sarah began to think of life not as a straight line of progress but as a dance. A step forward, a step back. A pause. A turn.

Loss and gain weren't enemies. They were partners. One always gave rise to the other.

This shift in perspective softened her heart. Instead of bracing herself against loss as an enemy to fight, she began to see it as part of the rhythm of being alive. Painful, yes. But also purposeful.

The bakery dream might one day fail. A new friendship might fade. Another home might be left behind. But she could trust that each letting go would make space for something else, something she couldn't yet imagine.

Reflection for You

Look back at your own story. Loss and gain may feel like opposites, but what if they are part of the same cycle?

Exercise: Mapping the Cycle

- Draw a timeline of your life. Mark the major losses — relationships, jobs, homes, opportunities.
- Next to each, write what eventually came afterward, even if it took years. Did you grow in resilience? Did you discover a new passion? Did another relationship or opportunity appear?

- Look for patterns. Where has loss cleared space for growth, even when it didn't feel like it at the time?
- Write one sentence about how you can trust this cycle in the future. Example: "Even when I lose something important, I trust it will make space for what I need next."

A Different Kind of Trust

For Sarah, the lesson was not that loss stopped hurting, but that it no longer felt meaningless. It was part of a larger flow she could begin to trust.

When she stood at her counter in the bakery, dusted with flour, she sometimes thought back to her office desk, her old apartment, her Saturday coffees with Emma. She still missed them. But she also understood something she hadn't before: those chapters ended so new ones could begin.

Loss was not just something to endure. It was something to move with — like a dancer trusting the next step, even if she couldn't see the whole routine.

And in that trust, Sarah found a new kind of freedom.

Chapter 6

Love That Leaves

Long before Sarah lost her job, her apartment, or her Saturday mornings with Emma, she had already known a different kind of loss — the loss of love.

It had been three years since her breakup with Daniel, the man she once thought she would marry. Their relationship had lasted almost five years, stretching from her late twenties into her early thirties. They had built routines together — cooking dinner side by side, Sunday hikes, long talks about the future. Sarah had even imagined the color of the walls in the house they would one day buy.

When it ended, it wasn't with a dramatic fight. It was a slow unraveling, marked by unspoken words and mismatched priorities. Daniel wanted to travel constantly, chasing new experiences. Sarah craved roots, a home to build together. Neither was wrong, but they were no longer walking in the same direction.

The day he packed his bags, Sarah felt like the floor of her life had given way.

The Ache of Absence

At first, Sarah tried to keep busy, filling her calendar with friends and distractions. But grief has a way of slipping through the cracks. She found herself reaching for two coffee mugs instead of one, hearing a song and instinctively wanting to text him, walking by restaurants they had once loved and feeling her chest tighten.

What hurt most wasn't just losing Daniel. It was losing the version of herself that existed in that relationship — the woman who was "half of a couple," who had someone to call at the end of the day, who felt chosen.

"Who am I without him?" she scribbled in her journal, tears blurring the ink.

What Love Leaves Behind

Months later, Sarah noticed something surprising. The silence in her apartment was still heavy, but she began to hear her own voice more clearly in it.

She realized how often she had gone along with Daniel's plans, shelving her own dreams. She had followed him to places she didn't care for, laughed at jokes she didn't always find funny, softened her opinions to keep the peace.

Without him, the space felt unbearable at first. But slowly, it became freedom.

She signed up for a pottery class, something she had always wanted to try but never made time for. She reconnected with her cousin, who had felt neglected during the years she spent wrapped in Daniel's orbit. She cooked meals that were entirely hers — spicy, experimental, nothing she had to compromise on.

The absence hurt, yes. But it also gave her back pieces of herself she hadn't realized she had lost.

This rediscovery planted a seed. It wasn't the bakery dream yet, but it was the courage to choose herself — a courage that would later lead her to that rainy afternoon in the bakery.

Love's True Work

Sarah began to see that love, even when it ends, does not leave us empty-handed.

It teaches us. It shapes us. And when it leaves, it clears space — sometimes for new love, sometimes for deeper self-love, sometimes simply for growth.

What Daniel gave her was real: companionship, memories, lessons. What his leaving gave her was equally real: independence, rediscovery, and the strength to define who she was outsidc of a rclationship.

Both mattered. Both were gifts.

Reflection for You

Think of a love you've lost — a partner, a friend, someone you once leaned on deeply. The loss may have left a wound, but it may also have left behind something you carry forward.

Exercise: Love's Legacy

- Write down the name (or initials) of someone whose love you lost.
- Underneath, write two gifts that relationship gave you while it lasted.
- Then, write two gifts the loss itself gave you — lessons, freedoms, rediscoveries, or strengths.
- Reflect: How might this love, even in its absence, still be shaping you toward who you are becoming?

Carrying Love Forward

Sarah no longer ached for Daniel in the same way she once had. The wound softened into a scar — tender, but not raw. She could remember him with gratitude, not only pain.

What she learned was this: love that leaves is not wasted. It leaves behind imprints, lessons, and space. It clears the way for the next chapter, whether that chapter is about new relationships or a deeper relationship with yourself.

Sarah carried Daniel with her, not in the weight of longing, but in the quiet ways his presence had shaped her and his absence had freed her.

Loss in love, she realized, is not the end of love. It is another form of it – one that teaches us how wide, how deep, and how resilient the heart can be.

Chapter 7
Family Ties

The phone call came on a rainy afternoon. Sarah's mother's voice trembled as she spoke the words Sarah had been dreading: "Your grandmother passed this morning."

Her grandmother, June, had been a constant presence in Sarah's life. She wasn't just a relative – she was a safe place. June had taught Sarah how to braid her hair, sent handwritten birthday cards every year, made tea and listened without judgment when Sarah's teenage world fell apart over a bad grade or a broken crush.

When Sarah thought of "home," she thought of her grandmother's kitchen – the smell of cinnamon rolls, the hum of an old radio, the steady comfort of someone who loved her exactly as she was.

And now, that kitchen was empty.

The Hollow Chair

At the funeral, Sarah sat in the front pew and stared at the casket draped in flowers. She couldn't stop thinking of the chair at the kitchen table where June always sat, her hands folded neatly, her eyes twinkling as if she carried some private joy.

The grief was sharp, but so was the fear. Sarah felt unmoored. June had been the family's anchor, the one who held gatherings together, who called every Sunday, who remembered details others forgot. Without her, what would become of the family?

The absence was bigger than one person. It was the absence of a role, a glue, a rhythm.

What We Carry Forward

Weeks later, Sarah found herself in her grandmother's house with her mother and aunt, sorting through belongings. She picked up a faded recipe card written in June's looping script: *Cinnamon Rolls.*

Sarah pressed the card to her chest and cried. But then she smiled. She realized she didn't lose June completely – she carried her forward in stories, recipes, and habits that had seeped into her bones.

The following Sunday, Sarah invited her mother and cousin over. She baked cinnamon rolls using June's recipe. The kitchen filled with the same smell that once defined her childhood.

It wasn't the same as sitting in June's kitchen, but it was a continuation. A way of keeping the love alive.

Sarah realized that family loss doesn't erase connection. It changes it. What we lose in presence, we often gain in memory, in tradition, in the chance to become the one who carries forward the love we once received.

The Shifting Roles

Over time, Sarah noticed that losing her grandmother also shifted her own role in the family. She began calling her mother more often, sending birthday cards to cousins, suggesting Sunday dinners. She had resisted stepping into responsibility before, but now she saw that her grandmother's absence had made space for her to show up in a new way.

It wasn't about replacing June. It was about honoring her by embodying the love she had modeled.

This new role felt like a quiet echo of her bakery dream — a way of creating spaces where people could feel at home, connected by simple acts of care.

Reflection for You

Family ties are some of the strongest — and the most painful to lose. But even in absence, love remains.

Exercise: Carrying Family Forward

- Think of a family member you've lost, or one whose role in your life has changed.
- Write down three things they gave you — lessons, traditions, or simple moments of love.
- Ask yourself: How can I carry one of these forward into my own life or family?
    - Maybe it's cooking their signature dish.
    - Maybe it's making a phone call they would have made.
    - Maybe it's telling a story about them to keep their memory alive.

Sarah's Realization

As Sarah pulled another tray of cinnamon rolls out of the oven months later, she felt something shift. Her grandmother was gone, but she wasn't lost. She lived on in the scent of cinnamon, in the warmth of family gathered around a table, in Sarah's decision to keep love alive through action.

Loss in family, Sarah realized, doesn't only take away. It also asks: *What role will you play now?*

Her grandmother's absence had left an empty chair. But it also left an invitation – for Sarah to become part of the glue that held her family together.

Chapter 8

When the Body Speaks

Sarah had always thought of herself as resilient. She prided herself on pushing through — late nights at the office, weekends spent catching up on chores, even headaches brushed aside with painkillers and coffee. She carried her exhaustion like a badge of honor, proof that she was strong enough to keep going.

But one morning, her body refused to cooperate.

She woke with a heaviness in her chest, a fatigue so deep that even sitting up felt impossible. At first, she told herself it was nothing — maybe stress, maybe a cold. But when the fatigue lingered for weeks and simple tasks like climbing stairs left her breathless, she finally went to the doctor.

The tests came back: anemia, aggravated by years of poor nutrition, overwork, and lack of rest.

It wasn't life-threatening, but it was a wake-up call. For years, Sarah had treated her body like a machine. Now, the machine had spoken — and it was saying "no more."

The Silence of Forced Rest

At first, Sarah resisted. She hated the prescription: more rest, a slower pace, more mindful eating. She wanted to push through, to keep doing everything she always had.

But her body didn't negotiate. When she ignored the signals, the fatigue returned stronger. She was forced to spend afternoons lying on the couch, staring at the ceiling, frustrated at her own limitations.

In those moments of forced stillness, she confronted an uncomfortable truth: she had been measuring her worth by how much she could do. Slowing down made her feel useless. But maybe, she thought, this loss of energy was pointing to something deeper.

The Body as Teacher

As weeks passed, Sarah began to listen more closely. She noticed how certain foods left her drained, while others gave her strength. She noticed how ten minutes of stretching in the morning eased the tension she carried all day. She noticed how deep breathing steadied her when her thoughts spiraled.

Her body, she realized, had been speaking all along. She had just never listened.

The diagnosis, the fatigue, the loss of stamina — it wasn't a punishment. It was her body asking her to create space for care, balance, and presence.

This lesson wasn't just about physical health. It was about listening to herself — a skill that would later guide her to say "no" to draining obligations and "yes" to her bakery dream.

Redefining Strength

Sarah began to shift her definition of strength. It wasn't about pushing past pain or ignoring limits. True strength, she learned, was honoring her body's needs, respecting its boundaries, and giving it what it required to thrive.

She started small: cooking iron-rich meals, taking short evening walks instead of collapsing in front of the TV, setting an earlier bedtime. With each choice, she felt a little stronger — not in the "push harder" way, but in the steady, sustainable way.

Her health scare had taken something away: the illusion that she could run herself ragged forever. But it also gave her something back: a partnership with her body, a chance to treat it not as an enemy or a machine, but as a home.

Reflection for You

Your body carries your story. Every ache, every surge of energy, every moment of fatigue is a message.

Exercise: Listening to Your Body

- Take a few quiet minutes and scan your body from head to toe. Notice where you feel tension, where you feel lightness, where you feel nothing at all.
- Write down three signals your body has been sending you lately (tiredness, headaches, cravings, restlessness, energy spikes).
- For each signal, ask: *What might my body be asking for?* Rest? Nourishment? Movement? Gentleness?
- Choose one small act of care you can give your body today, like drinking water, stretching, or taking a nap.

Sarah's Realization

Months later, Sarah reflected on her health scare with gratitude. She didn't enjoy the exhaustion, the frustration, or the slow recovery. But she saw now that her body's "breakdown" was really a breakthrough – a way of demanding the care she had long denied it.

When the body speaks, it often speaks through loss — loss of energy, loss of ability, loss of control. But Sarah learned that even these losses make space. Space for listening. Space for healing. Space for a new relationship with the one home we never leave: our body.

Chapter 9
Learning to Listen

Sarah's health scare taught her that her body wasn't indestructible, but it also opened a door to a broader kind of listening. She began to wonder: what if listening wasn't just about physical signals, but about tuning into her inner voice — her instincts, her desires, her truth?

For years, she had drowned out that voice with busyness, expectations, and the need to please others. Now, she saw that listening was a skill — one that could guide her through the losses and toward what she truly needed.

Small Signals, Quiet Truths

Sarah noticed that when she rushed through meals, her mind felt scattered, her energy low. When she slowed down, savoring each bite, she felt grounded and clear.

She noticed that on days she stayed glued to her computer, her thoughts grew anxious, her shoulders tight. But when she took breaks to stretch, walk, or gaze out the window, her mind softened, her creativity stirred.

She noticed that when she stayed up late scrolling her phone, her sleep was restless, her dreams uneasy. But when she dimmed the lights, read a book, or lay in the dark listening to her breath, she woke with a quiet calm.

Her inner voice had always been speaking — through her body, her emotions, her fleeting thoughts. She had simply been too busy to hear.

The Balance She Never Knew She Needed

For years, Sarah equated "rest" with laziness. Productivity had been her measure of worth. But now she realized: rest wasn't indulgence. Rest was fuel.

The days she let herself nap, journal, or sit in the garden weren't wasted — they prepared her for the days she needed to show up with strength.

Balance, she saw, wasn't about perfect schedules or strict routines. It was about rhythm. Work and rest. Movement and stillness. Effort and ease. Just like breathing: inhale, exhale. Both necessary, both sacred.

This rhythm became a guide. When she felt pulled toward her old habit of overworking, she paused, listened, and chose differently — a choice that later gave her the clarity to pursue her bakery dream.

Redefining Her Relationship with Herself

Sarah began to see herself not as something to conquer, but as something to befriend.

When she looked in the mirror, she no longer only saw flaws — dark circles, scars, the softness of her stomach. She saw evidence of survival. Her body, her mind, her heart had carried her through every heartbreak, every late night, every loss.

They were asking not for perfection, but for partnership. And partnership meant listening.

Reflection for You

Your body, your emotions, your instincts are speaking all the time. The question is: are you listening?

Exercise: A Conversation with Yourself

- Find a quiet space and sit comfortably.
- Place your hand on your chest or stomach. Take a few slow breaths.
- Ask yourself (out loud or silently): *What do I need today?*
- Write down the first word or phrase that comes to mind — rest, connection, courage, quiet.

- Take one action to honor that need today, like calling a friend, taking a walk, or writing in a journal.

Sarah's Realization

One evening, Sarah stood in her kitchen sipping tea, her journal open in front of her. She wrote:

"For the first time, I feel like I'm not fighting myself. We're on the same side."

That realization filled her with a kind of peace she had never known.

Learning to listen didn't erase her challenges. It didn't prevent her from ever feeling lost again. But it gave her a new compass. Whenever she felt adrift, she could tune into her inner voice, and it would point her back to balance.

Loss had opened the door. Listening was what led her through.

Chapter 10

Masks We Wear

Sarah had always been good at playing roles.

At work, she was the reliable one – the one who stayed late, smiled through exhaustion, and never complained. With friends, she was the easygoing one – the one who said, "I'm fine," even when she wasn't. With her family, she was the peacemaker – the one who avoided conflict, smoothing things over so others wouldn't argue.

Each role was like a mask she wore, carefully crafted to fit the expectations around her. And for a long time, those masks seemed to work. They kept people happy. They kept life moving smoothly.

But after losing her job, her apartment, her health, and even her grandmother, Sarah noticed something unsettling: without the masks, she didn't know who she was.

The Fear of Being Seen

One evening, Sarah went to a dinner party with a group of acquaintances. She found herself slipping into her usual role: smiling, nodding, listening more than speaking. She laughed at jokes she didn't find funny. She avoided mentioning her job loss or her health scare.

By the end of the night, she felt drained, hollow. Walking home under the streetlights, she asked herself: *Why am I still pretending? Why am I still hiding?*

The truth scared her. She was afraid that if she let people see her real self — her doubts, her grief, her messy dreams — they might not accept her.

But another truth was beginning to emerge, too: wearing masks was costing her more than it was protecting her.

When the Mask Slips

It happened by accident.

One afternoon, Sarah met her cousin for coffee. Without planning to, she admitted, "I've been so tired lately. Sometimes I feel like I'm failing at everything."

To her surprise, her cousin didn't judge her. Instead, she said, "Me too. I've been struggling at work, and I didn't want to tell anyone."

In that moment of honesty, Sarah felt closer to her cousin than she had in years. The mask had slipped — and instead of rejection, she found connection.

The Cost of Pretending

As Sarah reflected, she realized that masks may protect us from rejection, but they also block us from intimacy. When we hide our struggles, we also hide the parts of us that others might love most — our truth, our vulnerability, our humanity.

Every mask she wore had once served a purpose. But now, they felt heavy. And she was tired of carrying them.

Reflection for You

We all wear masks — roles we've learned to play to fit in, to keep the peace, to feel safe. But sometimes, the masks begin to suffocate us.

Exercise: Naming Your Mask

- Think of one role or mask you often wear (the strong one, the funny one, the achiever, the caretaker).
- Write down what purpose this mask serves — what it protects you from.
- Then, write what it costs you — what part of your authentic self it hides.
- Ask yourself: *What small, safe moment could I let this mask slip?* Maybe it's

sharing a worry with a friend or saying "no" to an obligation.

Sarah's Realization

Sarah didn't throw all her masks away at once. She still found herself smiling through moments of discomfort or saying "fine" when she wasn't. But she began practicing honesty in small doses — with her cousin, with Emma over the phone, even with herself in her journal.

Each time she spoke truth, she felt lighter. Each time she let someone see her without the mask, she felt more real.

The loss of her old roles — employee, girlfriend, granddaughter — had felt devastating. But it also gave her the chance to ask a deeper question: *Who am I, really, when the masks fall away*?

For the first time in years, she was beginning to find out.

Chapter 11

Becoming Herself

The masks were falling away, piece by piece. And for the first time, Sarah wasn't just grieving who she used to be – she was beginning to imagine who she might become.

It wasn't a sudden transformation. There was no single morning when she woke up and declared, "This is the real me." Instead, it was a slow unfolding, like a flower opening to the sun.

Choosing for Herself

One Saturday, Sarah stood in front of her closet. For years, her wardrobe had been filled with "safe" choices – button-up shirts for work, dresses that looked polished, shoes that were practical but uninspired.

That day, she pulled out a bright yellow dress she had bought on impulse years ago but never worn. "Too loud," she had once told herself. But now, she slipped it on. She wore it to the farmers' market, and strangers smiled at her as she walked by.

She felt...alive. Not because others noticed, but because the dress reflected something inside her – a brightness she had kept hidden.

Becoming herself, she realized, wasn't about grand gestures. It was about small choices that aligned with who she truly was.

The Power of Saying No

Another shift came when she began saying "no."

When a former coworker asked her to help with a project "just as a favor," Sarah felt the old urge to say yes, to prove her worth, to avoid disappointing anyone. But her body tensed, and she remembered her promise to listen to herself.

So she said, gently but firmly, "No, I can't take that on right now."

Her heart pounded. She expected judgment or distance. Instead, her coworker simply said, "I understand."

In that moment, Sarah realized: every time she said "no" to something that drained her, she was saying "yes" to herself.

Redefining Identity

For years, Sarah's identity had been tied to roles: employee, girlfriend, granddaughter, friend. Losing those roles had left her feeling like a blank page.

But now, she began to see the blankness differently. It wasn't emptiness. It was possibility.

She was not only what others expected of her. She was a woman who loved baking, who painted in the quiet evenings, who found joy in gardening, who wore yellow dresses to the market. She was not a role to fill — she was a person becoming.

These small choices — the dress, the "no," the baking — were threads weaving her closer to her dream of a bakery, a life where she could create spaces of warmth and connection.

Reflection for You

Who are you when the masks fall away?

Exercise: Becoming Yourself

- Write down three things you do mostly to meet others' expectations (how you dress, what you say yes to, what you hide).
- Then, write down three small ways you could choose differently — in a way that reflects your true self.
    - Maybe it's wearing the outfit you secretly love.

    - Maybe it's admitting when you're tired.
    - Maybe it's sharing a dream you've been afraid to say out loud.
- Take one small step this week toward choosing for yourself, like wearing a bold color or saying "no" to an obligation.

Sarah's Realization

One evening, Sarah sat in her garden, sipping tea as the sun set. She wrote in her journal:

"For so long, I thought I had to be who others needed me to be. But I'm starting to see – I am enough, just as I am. Becoming myself isn't about arriving somewhere. It's about choosing, every day, to live in alignment with who I really am."

She smiled, closed her journal, and breathed deeply.

The journey of loss had stripped away so many roles, so many masks. But in that space, she had found something better: herself.

Chapter 12

The Sacred in the Everyday

Sarah had never thought of herself as particularly spiritual. She had grown up attending church with her grandmother, but after moving away, the habit faded. For years, her "faith" was little more than hurried prayers in moments of crisis and vague gratitude when things went well.

But in the season of loss, Sarah began to notice something she had overlooked: a quiet thread of meaning woven through the ordinary details of her life.

This wasn't about religion or grand rituals. It was about finding connection — to herself, to others, to the world around her — in the smallest moments.

A Garden Moment

One morning, Sarah was watering the small herb garden outside her apartment. The basil leaves glistened with dew, the lavender swayed gently in the breeze, and the air carried a freshness that made her pause.

For a moment, everything felt still. Time slowed. She wasn't thinking about her to-do list, her bank account, or her future. She was simply there — present, breathing, alive.

Tears filled her eyes, though she didn't know why. It felt like grace. Like love. Like something larger than herself was whispering, "You're okay. You're not alone."

The Everyday Altars

Sarah began to see these moments more often:

- The quiet peace of early morning light spilling across her kitchen table.
- The warmth of flour between her fingers as she kneaded dough.
- The sound of laughter shared with a friend on the phone.
- The hush of her own breath slowing before sleep.

She realized she didn't need a cathedral or a formal practice to touch meaning. The sacred was everywhere, hidden in the ordinary. Life itself was the altar.

These moments of presence were like the warmth she wanted her future bakery to embody — a space where people could pause, connect, and feel at home.

Redefining Connection

For Sarah, this sense of the sacred wasn't about dogma or answers. It was about noticing — pausing long enough to feel connected to something deeper, whether that was mindfulness, love, or simply the act of being alive.

She didn't claim to understand it fully. She didn't need to. What mattered was the pause, the recognition of beauty in the mundane.

Loss had stripped away her certainty, her stability, her control. But in that space, she discovered a different kind of grounding — a connection rooted in presence, not perfection.

Reflection for You

Meaning doesn't have to be grand or complicated. Sometimes it's about noticing what's already there — in a moment, a breath, a simple act.

Exercise: Finding Meaning in the Everyday

- Choose a simple daily activity (making coffee, walking, folding laundry).
- As you do it, slow down. Notice the sights, sounds, textures, and feelings.

- Ask yourself: *What feels meaningful about this moment?* Is it the warmth, the rhythm, the sense of being alive?
- Write down one ordinary moment this week that felt extraordinary when you paid attention, like the scent of coffee or the sound of birds.

Sarah's Realization

One evening, Sarah sat at her kitchen table, candle lit, a plate of cinnamon rolls cooling nearby. She thought of her grandmother, of Daniel, of Emma, of all the losses that had once felt unbearable. She felt the ache of missing them, but also the gift of the moment – warm light, sweet scent, the simple fact of being here.

She whispered, "Thank you." Not to anyone in particular. Just to life.

For the first time, she understood: meaning is not separate from the everyday. It is the everyday, seen with open eyes.

Chapter 13
Trusting the Mystery

Sarah liked answers. She always had. As a child, she peppered her parents with "why" questions until they grew weary. As an adult, she Googled symptoms, overanalyzed conversations, and built careful plans for the future.

Answers, for Sarah, meant safety. They meant control.

But loss had taught her a different truth: sometimes there are no answers. Sometimes the "why" never arrives.

The Question Without an Answer

After her grandmother's passing, Sarah often found herself asking, "Why now? Why this way? Why when I still needed her?"

No answer came. Just silence.

When Daniel left, she had wondered, "What did I do wrong? Could I have changed the outcome?"

Again, no answer.

And when her body forced her to slow down, she asked, "Why can't I keep up like everyone else? Why me?"

Still — silence.

At first, that silence felt cruel. But over time, Sarah began to see it differently. Maybe the silence wasn't absence. Maybe it was an invitation — not to solve, but to trust.

The Gift of Not Knowing

One evening, Sarah sat in her garden under a sky littered with stars. She marveled at their vastness, the way they shone light from millions of years ago. She thought of how much she didn't know — about the universe, about life, about her own path.

And instead of fear, she felt wonder.

Not knowing wasn't failure. It was mystery. And mystery, she realized, could be beautiful.

Answers bring closure. But mystery brings possibility — like the possibility of a bakery she couldn't yet fully envision, but trusted she would build one day.

Living the Questions

Sarah remembered a line from Rainer Maria Rilke's *Letters to a Young Poet*: "Be patient toward all that is unsolved in your heart and try to love the questions themselves."

She wrote in her journal:

"What if I don't need to have everything figured out? What if life is less about solving and more about living the questions, one step at a time?"

The more she leaned into mystery, the lighter she felt. The need for control softened. The pressure to "get it right" eased. She began to trust that even in uncertainty, she was still moving forward.

Reflection for You

We all face questions without answers. Instead of forcing them closed, what if we learned to live with them?

Exercise: Living the Questions

- Write down one question in your life that you don't have an answer to (Why did this happen? What's next? Am I enough?).
- Instead of solving it, write: "I don't have the answer yet, and that's okay."
- List one way you can live with the question this week — with curiosity, openness, or trust, like taking a small step without knowing the outcome.

Sarah's Realization

As Sarah closed her journal and looked again at the night sky, she whispered, "I don't need to know everything to keep going."

The losses had left her with more questions than answers. But in that space, she found a new strength: the ability to trust the mystery.

Life wasn't a puzzle to be solved. It was a story to be lived. And the unknown wasn't a threat — it was the very place where new beginnings were born.

Chapter 14

The Gift of Loss

When Sarah looked back on the last few years, it felt like staring at a patchwork quilt. Pieces of her life that once seemed torn apart had been stitched together into something unexpected.

She still remembered the ache of those first losses — the job, the apartment, the friendships, her grandmother, Daniel. At the time, each one had felt like the end of something essential, as though the ground beneath her had been pulled away.

But standing where she was now, Sarah could see the fuller picture. Each loss had cleared space. And in that space, something new had emerged.

What She Gained

Losing her job had freed her to rediscover baking, a passion that gave her joy and pointed her toward a dream.

Losing her apartment had made room for a simpler home and a garden that became her sanctuary.

Losing her friendship with Emma had led to painting, quiet nights of self-discovery, and eventually, new friendships through her culinary class.

Losing her grandmother had deepened her appreciation for life's fragility and the importance of carrying forward small rituals of love.

Losing Daniel had hurt deeply but had also taught her that her worth didn't depend on being chosen – it came from within.

Loss had not just taken. It had also given.

A New Lens

Sarah realized she no longer saw loss only as endings. She saw it as a teacher. A guide. Sometimes harsh, but always transformative.

She thought of how trees shed their leaves in autumn. The loss looks like death, but really, it's clearing space for rest, renewal, and the growth of spring. Her life had followed the same rhythm.

The gift of loss was not in the pain itself – she wouldn't pretend otherwise. The gift was in what came after: the clarity, the courage, the space to begin again.

Reflection for You

Think back on a loss you've faced. Maybe it's still raw, maybe it's far behind you.

Exercise: Finding the Gift

- Write down the loss in one sentence.
- Then, ask yourself: What space did this create in my life?
    - Maybe it gave you freedom.
    - Maybe it shifted your priorities.
    - Maybe it revealed strength you didn't know you had.
- Write one sentence about how that loss shaped who you are today.

Sarah's Realization

One evening, Sarah baked a loaf of bread and shared it with her neighbors. As they laughed around her small kitchen table, she looked at the scene and thought, *If I had held on tightly to everything I lost, I would never be here. I would never have found this version of me.*

She smiled.

The gift of loss wasn't about erasing the sorrow. It was about embracing the transformation.

Chapter 15
Living Forward

Sarah stood at the doorway of her little apartment, sunlight spilling across the floor. A tray of muffins cooled on the counter, ready to bring to her class. Her garden thrived outside, herbs and flowers swaying in the breeze. Inside, a painting half-finished rested on her easel.

It wasn't the life she had imagined years ago. In some ways, it was smaller. But it was also richer, fuller, truer.

She had lost so much. And yet, here she was — not broken, but remade.

Choosing to Keep Moving

Loss had taught Sarah that life would never be predictable. Jobs would change. Relationships would shift. Health would ebb and flow. Loved ones would leave, one way or another.

But instead of fearing these changes, she had learned to move with them. To trust the cycle. To keep walking forward, even when the path was uncertain.

Now, when she faced challenges, she no longer asked only, “Why me?” She asked, “What is this making space for?”

That single shift had become her compass.

Building a Life That Fits

Sarah no longer tried to force herself into molds that didn’t fit. She chose work that gave her joy, even if it wasn’t the most prestigious. She wore colors that made her feel alive. She surrounded herself with people who supported her growth.

Most importantly, she gave herself permission to keep becoming. To be unfinished. To let life shape her in ways she couldn’t predict.

Reflection for You

Living forward means carrying the lessons of loss into your daily life.

Exercise: Living Forward

- Think of one area of your life where you’ve been holding on to “what was.”
- Ask yourself: What would it look like to step forward instead of back?
- Choose one small action this week that reflects the person you’re becoming, like

signing up for a class or letting go of an old expectation.

Sarah's Realization

On the evening of her first community bake sale, Sarah set up a small table outside a local park. Neighbors gathered, tasting her bread, chatting, laughing. Someone asked if she'd ever thought about opening a bakery. She smiled.

"Maybe someday," she said. And for the first time, the idea didn't feel like a distant dream – it felt like a possibility.

As the sun dipped low and the crowd lingered, Sarah felt a deep, quiet peace.

Loss had been her teacher. Space had been her gift. And forward – forward was her choice.

Closing

This is Sarah's story. But it can also be yours.

Every loss you face holds within it the seed of renewal. Every ending can make space for a beginning.

The question isn't whether life will change – it will. The question is: when change comes, how will you choose to live forward?

Epilogue

The Space Is Yours

Sarah's story began with loss. Jobs, homes, relationships, loved ones — all slipping away until she felt stripped bare. At first, she believed the emptiness was a sign of failure. But as she walked through the ache, she discovered something else: the emptiness was not a punishment. It was an invitation.

Every loss created space. And in that space, she found herself — her passions, her voice, her courage, her connection to the everyday, her trust in mystery, her ability to live forward.

This story isn't just Sarah's. It belongs to you, too.

You may not share her exact experiences, but you know what it means to lose. To grieve. To wonder who you are without what you've held so tightly. And just like Sarah, you have the same choice: to see loss only as an ending, or to embrace it as a beginning.

Your Invitation

The space left by loss is not empty. It is fertile. It is waiting.

- What will you plant there?

- What dream, long shelved, might find its way into the light?
- What part of yourself, long hidden, is ready to be seen?

You don't need to have the answers now. You only need to step forward with openness, trusting that each loss carries within it a gift — not always visible right away, but waiting to be discovered.

Closing Words

As you close this book, take a breath. Place your hand over your heart.

Remind yourself: *Everything I lose creates space for everything I need.*

The space is here. The choice is yours.

What will you create?

PART II

REFLECTION & WORKBOOK

Appendix

Your Journey Through Loss and Renewal

Sarah's story showed you a path through loss – from the weight of what was to the possibility of what could be. This section is your space to walk that path. These exercises are designed to help you reflect on your own losses, embrace the spaces they leave, and step toward renewal. Take your time. You don't need to complete them all at once. Let them unfold as gently as Sarah's journey did.

Understanding Your Losses

1. **Naming the Loss**
    - Write about a recent loss (big or small).
    - What did it represent for you? (security, identity, love, stability)
    - How do you feel when you think about it now?

    Prompt: This loss meant...

2. **Holding On Too Long**

- Identify something you've been clinging to, even though it no longer fits.
- Why is it hard to release?
- What might you gain if you let go?

Prompt: If I loosen my grip on this, I might find...

Embracing the Space

3. **Sitting with the Void**
   - Choose a quiet moment in your day. Be still for 5–10 minutes.
   - What thoughts or emotions surface?
   - What surprises you about the space left behind?

   Prompt: When I sit with the void, I notice...

4. **Finding What Matters**
   - List three things you want right now.
   - For each, ask: What do I truly need beneath this want?

- What small step could you take this week toward meeting that deeper need, like writing a gratitude list or calling a friend?

Prompt: Beneath my want for ___, I discover my need for ___.

Living the Cycle

5. **Mapping the Cycle of Loss and Gain**
    - Draw a timeline of your life.
    - Mark your major losses. Then, note what came after — new opportunities, perspectives, or strengths.
    - What patterns do you notice?

    Prompt: After I lost ___, I eventually found ___.

6. **Becoming Yourself**
    - List three ways you've been living to meet others' expectations.
    - Write three small choices that would reflect your true self, like wearing a bold color or sharing a hidden dream.
    - Pick one to try this week.

Prompt: When I choose for myself, I feel...

The Inner Landscape

7. **Finding Meaning in the Everyday**
    - Reflect on a moment that felt quietly meaningful (a sunrise, laughter, stillness).
    - What made it special to you?
    - How can you create space for more moments like this, like pausing during a walk or savoring a meal?

Prompt: Meaning shows up for me when...

8. **Trusting the Mystery**
    - Write down a question you don't have an answer to.
    - Instead of solving it, reflect on how you can live alongside it.
    - What possibility might the unanswered question hold?

Prompt: Though I don't know ___, I can still ___.

Living Forward

9. **The Gift of Loss**
    - Look back on one loss with distance.
    - What strength, clarity, or freedom did it eventually bring?
    - How has it shaped who you are today?

Prompt: Because I lost ___, I grew in ___.

10. **Living Forward**
    - Where in your life are you still holding onto "what was"?
    - What small step could you take toward "what is becoming"?
    - Write one commitment to yourself about how you will live forward.

Prompt: I choose to live forward by...

Closing Reflection

Take a final page to write your own mantra – words that remind you, like Sarah's did, that loss creates space.

Examples:

- I am not broken; I am becoming.
- Every ending makes way for a beginning.
- The space left behind is where I will grow.

Prompt: My mantra is...

PART III

30-DAY GUIDED PRACTICE

Creating Space for What You Need

This 30-day practice integrates Sarah's lessons into your life. Each day offers a reflection, journal prompt, and action. Follow sequentially or as needed.

Week 1: Understanding Loss

Day 1 – *Naming the Loss*

- *Reflection:* Like Sarah's job loss, name a loss shaking your identity.
- *Journal:* This loss meant...
- *Action:* Write a letter to the loss (unsent).

Day 2 – *Feeling Emotions*

- *Reflection:* Sarah journaled her grief. Notice your emotions without judgment.
- *Journal:* My emotions about this loss are...
- *Action:* Name emotions aloud or in writing for five minutes.

Day 3 – *Letting Go*

- *Reflection:* Sarah clung to her apartment. What do you hold too tightly?

- *Journal:* I can release...
- *Action:* Let go of one item (e.g., donate clothes).

Day 4 – *What Remains*

- *Reflection:* Sarah found passions amid loss. What endures for you?
- *Journal:* I can rely on...
- *Action:* List three things you're grateful for (e.g., a friend).

Day 5 – *Presence*

- *Reflection:* Sarah found peace in her garden. Pause to notice.
- *Journal:* A moment I noticed today was...
- *Action:* Take a 10-minute distraction-free walk.

Day 6 – *Your Needs*

- *Reflection:* Sarah needed purpose, not just a job. What do you need?
- *Journal:* Beneath my wants, I need...
- *Action:* Act on one need (e.g., nap, call a friend).

Day 7 – *Weekly Reflection*

- *Reflection:* How did naming loss shift your view, like Sarah's journaling?
- *Journal:* An insight about loss is...
- *Action:* Share an insight with a friend or journal.

Week 2: Embracing Space

Day 8 – *The Void*

- *Reflection:* Sarah painted in silence. The void is fertile.
- *Journal:* In quiet, I notice...
- *Action:* Sit in silence for 5–10 minutes.

Day 9 – *Joy*

- *Reflection:* Sarah's bakery visits sparked joy. What lights you up?
- *Journal:* A joy I want is...
- *Action:* Do it (e.g., dance, bake).

Day 10 – *Passion*

- *Reflection:* Sarah rediscovered baking. What passion waits for you?
- *Journal:* A neglected passion is...

- *Action*: Explore it (e.g., research a class).

Day 11 – Body's Voice

- *Reflection*: Sarah's body demanded care. What does yours say?
- *Journal*: My body tells me...
- *Action*: Respond (e.g., stretch, hydrate).

Day 12 – Emotional Release

- *Reflection*: Sarah let go of nostalgia. What weighs you down?
- *Journal*: I can release this memory...
- *Action*: Write and discard it safely.

Day 13 – Loss's Gift

- *Reflection*: Sarah found purpose in loss. What gift did yours bring?
- *Journal*: My loss gave me...
- *Action*: Share it (e.g., tell a friend).

Day 14 – Weekly Reflection

- *Reflection*: How has space changed you, like Sarah's painting?
- *Journal*: I discovered...

- *Action:* Light a candle in gratitude.

Week 3: Building Identity & Resilience

Day 15 – *Your Masks*

- *Reflection:* Sarah hid behind roles. What masks do you wear?
- *Journal:* A mask I wear is...
- *Action:* Drop it once (e.g., share a struggle).

Day 16 – *Authentic Choices*

- *Reflection:* Sarah wore a yellow dress. What choice reflects you?
- *Journal:* A choice true to me is...
- *Action:* Make it (e.g., wear bold colors).

Day 17 – *Saying No*

- *Reflection:* Sarah said "no" to draining favors. Where can you set boundaries?
- *Journal:* I can say no to...
- *Action:* Politely decline one obligation.

Day 18 – *Redefining Strength*

- *Reflection:* Sarah saw strength in care, not pushing. What's your strength?

- *Journal:* My strength lies in...
- *Action:* Honor it (e.g., rest, create).

Day 19 – Intuition's Guide

- *Reflection:* Sarah trusted her intuition for balance. What does yours say?
- *Journal:* My intuition tells me...
- *Action:* Follow it (e.g., pause when tired).

Day 20 – Connection

- *Reflection:* Sarah found connection in honesty. Where can you connect?
- *Journal:* I feel connected when...
- *Action:* Reach out (e.g., call a friend).

Day 21 – Weekly Reflection

- *Reflection:* How has authenticity shaped you, like Sarah's choices?
- *Journal:* I'm becoming...
- *Action:* Write your personal mantra.

Week 4: Living Forward

Day 22 – Everyday Meaning

- *Reflection*: Sarah found sacredness in basil, dough. Where's yours?
- *Journal*: Meaning shows up in...
- *Action*: Slow a task (e.g., savor coffee).

Day 23 – Trusting Mystery

- *Reflection*: Sarah embraced unanswered questions. Can you?
- *Journal*: An unanswered question is... It's okay because...
- *Action*: Act without certainty (e.g., try a new hobby).

Day 24 – Loss's Lessons

- *Reflection*: Sarah's losses taught resilience. What did yours teach?
- *Journal*: My loss taught me...
- *Action*: Share the lesson (e.g., write a story).

Day 25 – *Forward Steps*

- *Reflection:* Sarah chose forward. What step can you take?
- *Journal:* I can move forward by...
- *Action:* Take it (e.g., sign up for a class).

Day 26 – *Building Your Life*

- *Reflection:* Sarah built a life of joy. What does yours look like?
- *Journal:* My life feels true when...
- *Action:* Create it (e.g., declutter, plan).

Day 27 – *Resilience*

- *Reflection:* Sarah trusted the cycle. How can you?
- *Journal:* I trust my resilience because...
- *Action:* Face a small challenge with courage.

Day 28 – *Weekly Reflection*

- *Reflection:* How has living forward felt, like Sarah's bake sale?
- *Journal:* I've grown by...

- *Action:* Celebrate with a small ritual (e.g., bake).

Day 29 – *Your Space*

- *Reflection:* Sarah's losses made space. What will you create?
- *Journal:* In my space, I will...
- *Action:* Start it (e.g., sketch a dream).

Day 30 – *Closing Commitment*

- *Reflection:* Sarah chose herself. What's your commitment?
- *Journal:* I commit to...
- *Action:* Write and display your mantra.

Closing Encouragement

Loss will come — it is part of life's rhythm. But in the spaces left behind, there is opportunity. Every ending creates room for beginnings, for growth, and for self-discovery.

The space is yours. What will you create?

9 788199 262379

Printed at Repro India Ltd.